NIAGARA DAREDEVILS

AMAZING STORIES

NIAGARA DAREDEVILS

Thrills and Spills Over Niagara Falls

HISTORY/ADVENTURE

by Cheryl MacDonald

PUBLISHED BY ALTITUDE PUBLISHING CANADA LTD.
1500 Railway Avenue, Canmore, Alberta T1W 1P6
www.altitudepublishing.com
1-800-957-6888

Extreme care has been taken to ensure that all information presented in
this book is accurate and up to date. Neither the author nor the
publisher can be held responsible for any errors.

Publisher	Stephen Hutchings
Associate Publisher	Kara Turner
Editor	Frances Purslow
Digital photo colouring & map	Scott Manktelow

We acknowledge the financial support of the Government
of Canada through the Book Publishing Industry Development
Program (BPIDP) for our publishing activities.

Altitude GreenTree Program 🌲
Altitude Publishing will plant twice as many trees as were used
in the manufacturing of this product.

National Library of Canada Cataloguing in Publication Data
MacDonald, Cheryl, 1952-
Niagara daredevils / Cheryl MacDonald

(Amazing stories)
Includes bibliographical references
ISBN 1-55153-962-4

1. Stunt men and women--Niagara Falls (N.Y. and Ont.)--Biography.
2. Niagara Falls (N.Y. and Ont.)--Biography. I. Title. II. Series: Amazing
stories (Canmore, Alta.)
FC3095.N5M31 2003   971.3'390099   C2003-910897-X
F127.N8M31 2003

An application for the trademark for Amazing Stories™
has been made and the registered trademark is pending.

Printed and bound in Canada by Friesens
2 4 6 8 9 7 5 3

Front cover: Anna Edson Taylor, the first person
to go over Niagara Falls in a barrel.
(Reproduced courtesy of Niagara Falls (Ontario) Public Library.)

For my nephew Max MacDonald Schlesinger —
like Niagara Falls he has a history in both
Canada and the United States

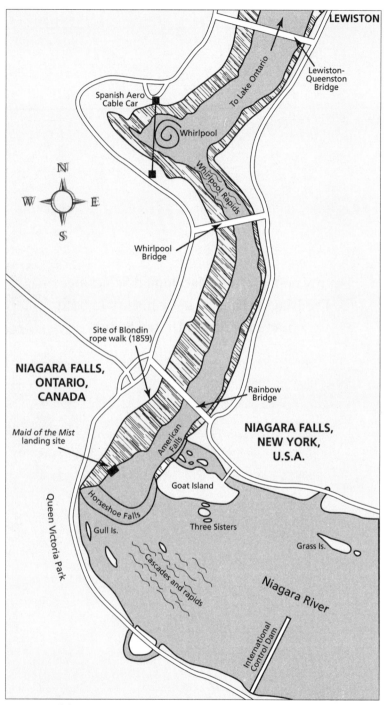

A map of the Niagara River at Niagara Falls showing the major features

Contents

Prologue

Wearing a long black dress with lacy cuffs and a large black hat, Anna stepped aboard the boat. She was rowed to Grass Island, where, hidden behind some bushes, she shed the outer garments and emerged hatless, clothed in a short skirt, blue and white blouse and light slippers. The plump, 63-year-old widowed school teacher moved towards the river, where Fred Truesdale and William Holloran, the rivermen she had hired for the day, helped her into a sturdy oak barrel. She strapped on the harness designed to keep her from moving around, then cushions were stuffed between her body and the walls and between her head and the lid.

Once Billy Holloran had pumped extra air into the barrel, Fred Truesdale rowed it out to the middle of the river. Then he heard a weak knock. Annie called out that water was leaking into the barrel.

Determining that the leak was small, Truesdale assured her that there was no cause for worry. Then he cut her loose.

Niagara Daredevils

Hundreds of eyes were glued to the barrel, a "dark speck rushing with lightning wings towards the centre of the great horseshoe of water." Then the crowd gasped as the barrel plunged over the falls and disappeared in a cloud of mist.

Chapter 1
Swimmers and Jumpers

iagara, in the words of Father Louis Hennepin, the French missionary who first described it in 1678, is "an incredible cataract or waterfall, which has no equal." There are actually three falls: the American Falls, and on the Canadian side Luna Falls (also known as the Bridal Veil) and Horseshoe Falls. The American Falls are 64 metres high, the Canadian 54. Every minute, approximately 14 million litres of water roar over the three cataracts.

From colonial times, Niagara Falls was a popular tourist destination. Many were content simply to gaze upon the falls, but others, such as English writer Oscar Wilde, were unimpressed. Wilde, who visited in 1882, called the falls "the second major disappointment of American married life ... vast unnecessary amounts of water going the wrong way and then falling over unnecessary rocks. The wonder would be if the water did not fall." Others wanted something more than a natural wonder. They wanted a show, a spectacle that pitted human skill and ingenuity against the water's awesome power. And, almost from the beginning, there were men (and a handful of women) ready to meet the challenge

Sam Patch was the first of the 19th century Niagara daredevils. According to journalist (and future 1837 rebellion leader) William Lyon Mackenzie, his first plunge was off Passaic Falls, New Jersey, "with the view of getting rid of the cares and troubles of life." He was 20 at the time and had just been rejected by a young woman he admired. Having survived, the slim, dark-haired former sailor and mill worker continued to take the plunge for just about anyone who asked. In 1829, looking for a stunt that would draw crowds, a group of Niagara Falls, New York businessmen invited him to town. The businessmen also planned to blow up a large section of Table Rock, but were talked out of it by authorities worried that it might change the course of the river and drain the Welland Canal, a vital transportation corridor. Sam's stunt, however, went ahead.

A 38-metre ladder was mounted over the gorge, downstream from Goat Island and across from the Cave of the Winds. Part way up — the height was variously given as 26 or 36 metres — was a small platform over which fluttered the American flag. Sam's jump was scheduled for noon, but shortly after 11 A.M. a chain holding the ladder to the cliff wall snapped. Five metres of ladder were torn away and the jump was postponed until 4 P.M.

It had been raining and there was a heavy mist, but by three o'clock crowds were gathered on both sides of the river. Promptly at four, Sam appeared, wearing a black vest and white trousers. He acknowledged his audience, moved forward, took a deep breath and jumped, holding his arms more or less in front of him and his feet slightly apart.

Down he plunged, hitting the water feet first with a great splash and "disappeared like a stone." For several agonizing seconds there was no sign of him. Then his head emerged above the water, and he swam for shore on his back.

"Sam Patch has immortalized himself," trumpeted Mackenzie's newspaper, the *Colonial Advocate.*

But there was no question of Sam sitting back and enjoying his fame. A short time later he was off to Rochester to jump off the 30-metre Genessee Falls. He built a platform, practised a few jumps privately, then scheduled a public jump for November 6, 1829. Sam, "a greater friend to the bottle than the bottle is to him," according to Mackenzie, visited several taverns immediately before his Rochester plunge. Then he climbed the platform, threw his pet bear cub in and prepared to follow.

Eyewitnesses disagreed on whether he jumped or fell. Instead of going into the water feet first, he apparently hit it full length. There was a loud impact, Sam disappeared below the surface and never came up. His body was found the following spring.

Like Elvis Presley, Sam Patch was so famous that many refused to believe he had died. People reported seeing and talking to him and his comment, "Some things can be done as well as others," became a popular saying. Sam's youth and crowd-pleasing bravado persuaded many that he had somehow survived. But there was no doubt about the fate of another Niagara daredevil, Captain Matthew Webb.

Born in Dawley, England in 1848, Webb learned to swim early. As a boy he saved his brother from drowning in the Severn River. As an apprentice sailor on the Mersey River, he saved a shipmate from drowning. His career gave him many opportunities to exercise his skill in swimming and diving, skills Webb stressed, that were important for safety. Once in South Africa he dived into rough waters to carry a lifesaving line to a ship wrecked on a shoal. In 1873, while stationed aboard the Cunard steamship *Russia*, he risked his own life by plunging into the water to save a shipmate who had fallen into the icy North Atlantic.

That feat won him the first gold medal presented by Britain's Royal Humane Society. The resulting publicity led more or less directly to a career change. Although he had his captain's papers, Webb decided to give up the sea-faring life to pursue a career as a professional swimmer.

Because relatively few people could swim, the sport focussed more on exhibitions, competitions between a handful of professionals, and setting new records. On July 3, 1874, Webb set a record in a 20-metre swim that stood unbroken until 1899. The next year, he became the first man to swim the English Channel, making the crossing from Dover to Calais in 21 hours and 45 minutes.

Already celebrated for his lifesaving feats, Captain Webb became a national hero. The London

Daily Telegraph proclaimed him, "The best known and most popular man in the world." He toured extensively, lecturing about his sport. He wrote a book titled *The Art of Swimming*. Always he emphasized safety and endurance, pointing out that in a shipwreck, the swimmer who stayed afloat longest would be most likely to be rescued.

Prize purses and public appearances on both sides of the Atlantic paid well. Soon it seemed there was nothing Webb would not attempt, from floating in a tank at the Boston Horticultural Show for 128 hours to imitating dolphins for hotel guests during a pyrotechnic display. But by the time he was in his early 30s, Webb's prowess had begun to decline. Younger swimmers were coming on the scene, and his endurance was not what it had once been. During one race in 1881 he collapsed, spitting blood.

Although he recovered, a hint of desperation crept into Webb's activities, especially after he married and started a family. Something of a spendthrift, he became obsessed with making money. Where better to seek a fortune than the legendary Niagara Falls?

When Webb announced his intentions to swim the rapids and whirlpool in the Niagara gorge just below the falls, colleagues and the general public were horrified. The water in the rapids, which

Matthew Webb, champion swimmer

stretched almost half a kilometre, raced by at 63 kilometres per hour, and the whirlpool spun so dizzily that there was no hope of rescuing him should his strength fail. The plan was suicidal! In fact, one Niagara Falls constable threatened to arrest him for attempted suicide. But Webb would not be deterred. "Don't care. I want money and must have it."

In the late 19th century, savvy promoters often made money by striking a deal with railway companies for a share of the increased revenue a special event could generate. In Webb's case, the railways weren't interested. Newspapers hesitated to publicize a stunt that seemed doomed to tragedy. Still Webb persisted. As he told reporters, "I am doing it because no other man has made an attempt. I am determined that my reputation shall not suffer."

On July 24, 1883, a few hours before his attempt, reporters described Webb. "The lines of the face were sternly drawn, an occasional drop of perspiration would gather on his brow, and his words ... had an earnestness that was almost solemn." Only a few hundred spectators turned out to watch the champion of the English Channel risk his life in a foolhardy attempt to restore his celebrity status. Shortly after 4 P.M. he walked down the hill from Clifton House to a waiting boat. Although McCloy, his boatman, tried at the last minute to talk him out of it, Webb was adamant. At 4:20 P.M., moments after passing under the suspension bridge, Matthew Webb stood up in the boat. He was wearing his trademark red silk diving costume, just as he had during his Channel crossing.

Webb had told a reporter from the *Toronto Globe* a few hours earlier, that he was not certain when he would hit rough water, or how he would handle it. "There is no place in the world like it, and I am trusting to fortune." His strategy, he told the reporter, was to be carried by the current, using his strength only to keep his head above the surface.

Webb dived into the water and for the first few minutes he was seen swimming strongly.

Then he entered the rapids and seemed to stand upright momentarily. For a quarter of an hour he bobbed out of sight and back into view repeatedly before entering the whirlpool. Then his arms shot up and he vanished.

The spot where "Poor Captain Webb" was last seen alive was pointed out to travellers for years to come. On July 27, his body was found between Lewiston and Youngston. His side and thigh were gashed, his skull exposed, and the famous red swimsuit torn to pieces. He was buried in Oakwood Cemetery, close to the falls.

In 1908, 60 years after his birth, Webb's hometown of Dawley installed a monument in his memory. The inscription read, "Nothing Great is Easy." Despite (or maybe because of) his tragic death, Matthew Webb's message of safety apparently got through to some swimmers, including William Kendall, an athletic 24-year old. On August 22, 1886, the Boston policeman checked into Sault's hotel in Niagara Falls, New York. After lunch he hired a cab, brought Frank Sault along and had the driver head for the *Maid of the Mist* landing. When he told the driver that he was going to swim the rapids on a bet, the cabbie replied, "You must be crazy!"

Kendall calmly showed him a canvas vest lined with five thick cork squares. At 2 P.M., Kendall stripped, donned the vest, and plunged into the rapids in "a long, deep dive." Although a strong swimmer, Kendall was tossed about by the water and sometimes disappeared completely beneath the churning surface. At the whirlpool, he vanished completely. When he emerged some distance away, he was unconscious.

Fortunately the life jacket kept him afloat as he drifted along for a short distance. Then he was sucked underwater again. This time, the water seemed to clear his head. He struck out for shore, hauled himself onto some rocks, and was pulled to safety by a couple of men. By the time he downed a glass of whisky, his cab had arrived. Kendall was taken to the Waverly House and examined by a doctor, who found no permanent damage. According to the *Globe* reporter who interviewed him, the young policeman had bet $100 that he could swim the rapids, while friends in Boston had wagers amounting to $10,000 on the feat. "The trip," he said, "nearly killed him, and no amount of money would tempt him to repeat it." He returned to Boston the following day.

Kendall was one of a handful of men to deliberately imitate Matthew Webb by swimming the rapids and whirlpool as a publicity stunt. Sam Patch, also had a few imitators. Lawrence Donovan made a jump from the Upper Suspension Bridge on November 7, 1886. At the time he was wearing a suit, canvas shoes, and a bowler hat. He survived to jump off the Brooklyn Bridge the following year. I. Ashley didn't exactly jump, but on May 3, 1890 he lowered himself from the suspension bridge with an aluminum tape.

Eighteen years later, Bobby Leach, an English circus performer, made several jumps. The first, from the Upper Steel Arch Bridge, took place on July 1, 1908. Leach jumped from a platform especially built for his stunt and wore a parachute, which opened after he dropped 15 metres. About 3 metres above the water, he removed the parachute and harness, dropped into the river, and swam to a waiting boat. Leach emerged unscathed, although a spectator attending a street railway convention in Niagara Falls was slightly injured when a pole supporting the platform fell on his head. Leach went on to make two jumps into the river from an airplane, in 1920 and 1925. Another man, Vincent Taylor, jumped from the Upper Steel Arch Bridge in 1927.

The jumpers got some attention, but none ever rivalled Sam Patch. Possibly the public was a little jaded by the time Sam's successors came along. They wanted more spectacle, more prolonged risks, a real battle between man and the elements. Although there was no doubt the risks were real, jumps were over all too quickly. In contrast, there was a certain fascination in seeing a daredevil right in the water, pitting his (or occasionally, her) wits and skill against the power of Niagara's rushing torrent. While no one really expected a repetition of Webb's or Kendall's swim, there were plenty of spectators who eagerly turned out to watch other daredevils try their luck.

Chapter 2
The Funambulists

iagara's very first tightrope walker was Jean François Gravelet, better known as Charles Blondin. In the summer of 1858, he was touring with a group of circus acrobats. Along the way they visited Niagara Falls where, the story goes, Blondin remarked to a companion that the gorge would be a spectacular place to string a tightrope.

His companion scoffed, but Blondin had already fallen under Niagara's spell. The following year he returned, determined to make a name for himself by crossing a tightrope high above the Niagara River.

In fact, Blondin already enjoyed a modicum of fame. Born in St. Omer, in northern France, in 1824, he was so fascinated by a performance he saw as a young child, that he began practising in his yard. His father, a gymnast himself, encouraged the boy, and at the tender age of five, young Jean François was enrolled in a gymnastic school in Lyons. A short time later, he gave his first performance, billed as "The Little Wonder."

By the time he was nine, Jean François was orphaned and forced to turn professional to support himself. Hired by a touring company, he changed his name to avoid confusion with two colleagues, the Javell brothers.

Blondin was a seasoned performer when he launched his career at Niagara Falls. Fair-haired and sporting a neat goatee, he weighed about 140 pounds, all of it muscle. His small frame housed an enormous ego, a useful quality for a daredevil performer but something of a hindrance when negotiating. His first attempts to arrange a venue for his act failed, because certain Niagara Falls residents didn't care for his attitude. Initially, he hoped to have his tightrope strung at Goat Island, above the falls, but the owner refused permission. Blondin had already made it clear that he, not the falls, would be the focus of the spectacle. Niagara was simply a dramatic back-drop for his performance.

While some people worried that Blondin would trivialize the falls, others recognized the income potential. Eventually he persuaded operators of two tourist attractions — White's Pleasure Grounds on the American side and Clifton House on the Canadian — to allow him to perform. They would charge admission, Blondin would pass the hat after each performance, and the visitors would see a spectacular show.

Crowds were attracted to Blondin's performance because of the risk factor. One slip might mean disaster, and that everpresent danger enhanced the thrill for many visitors. But behind the scenes Blondin did everything in his power to guarantee his own safety. His rope was 7.5 centimetres in diameter, strongly woven from manila hemp fibres. Measuring 33.5 metres long, it was stabilized with a series of 44 guy ropes at each end, all lashed down to posts and trees to keep the tightrope from swaying.

With years of performing under his belt, Blondin knew just how to draw a crowd. He hired a manager, Harry Colcord, and promoted the event extensively. On June 30, 1859 he was ready for his first walk. The rope was strung between what is now Oakes Garden on the Ontario side and the present-day Prospect

Park in New York state. Wearing an outlandish costume — a dark wig, purple vest, and billowing Turkish trousers, Blondin strolled over to the rope around five in the afternoon. Removing wig, vest and trousers, he pulled himself onto the tightrope and, using a 9-metre pole for balance, slowly eased out over the gorge.

All eyes were fixed on him as he moved farther and farther out from land and safety. Then a gasp went up as he stopped, produced a bottle, and lowered it with a piece of twine to the *Maid of the Mist* on the river below. After someone on the boat filled the bottle with river water, Blondin hauled it up, took a long drink, and proceeded on his way. Reaching the Canadian side, he drank a small glass of champagne, performed a little dance on the tightrope, and returned to the American side within 8 minutes. The whole performance, which was witnessed by thousands, took about 20 minutes.

Blondin's daring and cool demeanour made him an instant celebrity. The *New York Times* called his stunt "the greatest feat of the Nineteenth Century." But Blondin was not about to stop with a single crossing. More importantly, he was enough of a showman to know that audiences would quickly grow bored with a simple repeat of his first crossing. So he brought variety to every performance. He crossed on a bicycle, blindfolded, with his hands and feet manacled. On one crossing, he carried a small cook stove, stopped midway, fried up two omelettes, and lowered them to the *Maid of the Mist*. The passengers pushed and shoved as they fought for a souvenir piece or a taste of the meal cooked by the "Prince of Manila."

During the 1859 season alone, Blondin crossed the Niagara River on tightrope nine times. The most spectacular performance of that season occurred on August 19, when Blondin decided to carry his manager, Harry Colcord, on his back. Blondin was in top physical form, but Harry outweighed him by five pounds. Although the guy ropes kept the tightrope reasonably stable near the shore, in the middle the rope swayed dangerously. As Blondin moved into the centre of the rope, it seemed he was in terrible danger. Time and time again he told Colcord to get down, so he could rest. Then, as they approached the far side, Blondin put out his hand to steady himself by grasping a guy rope. It broke. For a moment it seemed both men would plunge to a watery death.

Thinking quickly, Blondin rushed to the next guy rope. This time it held. After catching his breath, the men continued. The crowds, in a near frenzy from

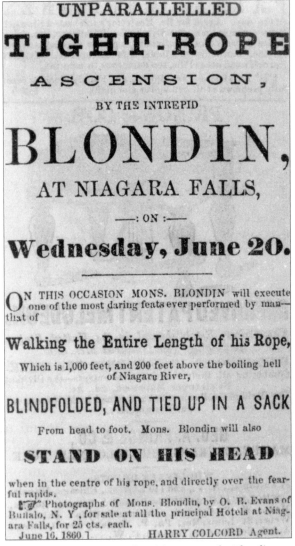

A poster from 1860 advertising a stunt by Blondin

excitement, were pressing to the very edge of the precipice. Blondin and Colcord realized that something had to be done or they could be swept into the water by the oncoming crowd. After a hurried consultation, they decided Blondin should run into the crowd at the last moment. He did so, and both men survived.

For months afterwards, Harry Colcord swore he had nightmares about the crossing. Perhaps he did, but more than likely it was a publicity ploy, since Blondin took Colcord across on two more occasions.

When it came to drawing crowds, almost nothing was taboo. On one occasion, Blondin persuaded a marksman, Captain John Travis, to shoot a hole through his hat as he stood in the middle of the tightrope. Travis aimed his pistol from the deck of the *Maid of the Mist*. The crowds were awed at the skill demonstrated by both men — the marksman, on a boat that heaved up and down in the roaring waters of the Niagara River, and the funambulist on the swaying rope high above. Then there was a loud gunshot, Blondin removed his hat and lowered it to the *Maid of the Mist*, where spectators clearly saw a hole in the centre. In fact, Travis had fired a blank, and Blondin had put the hole in the hat himself.

Still, the occasional sleight of hand did nothing

to diminish Blondin's performance. So great was his fame that when the Prince of Wales (the future King Edward VII) toured Canada in 1860, he stopped at Niagara Falls to watch Blondin perform. For the royal performance, Blondin walked across the tightrope on stilts. Then, putting the stilts aside, he crossed the tightrope carrying his assistant, Romain Mouton. When he was presented to the Prince, Blondin offered to take him across the tightrope, either on his back or in a wheelbarrow, "Thank you, but not today," the Prince reputedly replied. He did, however, present the daredevil with a purse containing £100. And, according to some reports, he asked Blondin never to undertake such a dangerous performance again. But that didn't stop him from requesting Blondin appear at a command performance at Crystal Palace in London, England in 1861. This time, Niagara Falls was depicted with a painted backdrop.

At this point, Blondin had already said goodbye to the real Niagara Falls forever. Although he still walked the tightrope in public, he would never again risk his life near the falls that had made him famous. The Prince of Manila continued performing until his late 60s, having become a very wealthy man. He died in bed in his home in England at the age of 73.

Blondin's Niagara Falls appearance capped his

career as a high-wire artist. But one man presented a serious challenge to his supremacy — a Canadian resident whose sojourn as a Niagara daredevil was just one chapter in a colourful career.

William Leonard Hunt was born in Lockport, New York in 1838, but was raised in Port Hope, Ontario. The son of an English immigrant, he fell in love with the circus at an early age and began honing his own skills. His father disapproved. Like many respectable people of the time, he looked down on performers, and especially circus performers, as low-class and immoral.

Yet nothing stopped young Will Hunt. As he later wrote, he was always in trouble of some kind. At one point, he staged his own circus with friends, a performance that enraged their parents and may have led Port Hope council to ban circus performances three years later.

Will's parents arranged for him to study with a local doctor, hoping he would pursue an appropriate career. Will had other plans. He was already strong enough to lift 700 pounds and had mastered the skill of tightrope walking. In 1859, when Will's father was away on a prolonged vacation, the local newspaper editor talked him into performing at a local fair. Initially offered $100, 21-year-old Will negotiated a

$500 fee — more than many men earned in a year. The editor gave in, on one condition: Will had to stand on his head above the Ganaraska River. Over 8000 people turned out to watch his performance, which brought him a taste of fame. Will changed his name to Signor Guillermo Antonio Farini, soon to be billed as "The Great Farini." When his father returned from England he was furious, convinced Will had disgraced the family. A short time later, the young man left home for good.

He drifted around the American Mid-West holding a series of jobs, including one as a tightrope walker with a travelling circus. By 1860, he was working as a store clerk in Lockport, New York and was engaged to the boss's daughter. That summer after seeing Blondin perform, Farini announced he could do as well, and quit his job. His girlfriend promptly ended their engagement.

For some time, Farini had been issuing challenges to Blondin, all of which were ignored. Finally, on August 15, 1860, the Great Farini made his Niagara Falls debut.

Farini's "First Ascension across the Niagara River" was widely advertised. He was a canny businessman, who worked feverishly to guarantee a large audience and substantial profits. The publicity for

Farini crossing the Niagara River on a tightrope

the August 15th performance was designed to tantalize audiences by offering a spectacle even more audacious than those provided by Blondin, at an admission price of 25¢, or 50¢ for reserved seats. Along with standing on his head, lying at full length on his back, and hanging by his heels and toes from the rope, Farini also promised the "Most Daring Feat ever Witnessed in the World."

True to his word, Farini provided a death-defying show. Holding his balance pole, the muscular young man walked onto the tightrope with a coil of rope strapped to his back. At mid-point he stopped, tied the pole to the tightrope, then uncoiled the rope and lowered himself to the deck of the *Maid of the Mist,* some 46 metres below. On the deck of the steamer, Farini enjoyed a quick glass of wine and started back up. But the man who had once single-handedly defeated a dozen men in a tug-of-war found the journey back to the tightrope almost beyond his strength. Exhausted, he nearly fell several times, but persevered and eventually made it back to the tightrope. After reaching the far shore, he rested briefly before putting baskets on his feet and a blindfold over his eyes and walking back.

Between admission fees, percentages of railway and excursion boat fares, and a collection taken up by spectators, Farini brought in close to $15,000 for his first Niagara performance. Although he would never repeat the nearly disastrous climb to the river and back again, he continued to thrill audiences with entertaining daring performances. As biographer Shane Peacock has written, "Farini's forté was terror and inventiveness." He also seems to have had a more highly developed sense of humour than Blondin. One of his most popular characters was Biddy O'Flaherty, the Irish washerwoman, a stock figure in literature and popular culture at the time. On September 5, 1860, Farini appeared as Biddy, dressed in women's clothing and a fancy hat and carrying a washing machine, basically a large tub that weighed 100 pounds. The women's clothing did nothing to disguise Farini's sex appeal. Long a favourite with the ladies, with whom he carried on a series of flirtations and brief romances, Farini graciously accepted the handkerchiefs they offered him before he made his tightrope crossing as Biddy.

Then he set off with his tub. At the centre of the tightrope, he fastened the tub in place with a pole run through its centre, pulled out a pail and smaller rope from its interior, and lowered the pail to the river. Using river water he washed the handkerchiefs then set them to dry in a rig of cords before completing the journey and returning them to their admiring owners.

Although newspapers tended to devote more space to Blondin's feats, Farini was a more-or-less even match for him. Like Blondin, he carried a man across on his back, performed stunts in mid-stream, and travelled blindfolded or hampered by baskets on his feet or manacles on his hands.

Possibly the most stunning visual performance either man gave was in September 1860. While Blondin made his crossing pushing a wheelbarrow full of fireworks, Farini actually wore his illumination — four paper lamps attached to a pole and several "Farini candles," a type of firework. As he crossed, he was enveloped in the flicker of lights from the lamps and the candles. Then the candles exploded, and it seemed he was engulfed in flames. After reaching the Canadian side, he started back, this time without illumination. It was almost impossible to see him in the deepening gloom. Then, more then a kilometre away, one of Blondin's firecrackers went off, and for a moment both funambulists were visible in the pale light.

Farini eventually took his show on the road, travelling to various American and European cities. His last Niagara performance, on August 8, 1864, was a disaster. This time, rather than a tightrope act, he planned to walk to the brink of the American falls wearing a pair of specially constructed iron stilts. Midway through the performance, one of the stilts caught in rocks in the riverbed and broke. Hampered by a seriously injured leg, Farini struggled to Robinson Island, near Luna Falls, and awaited rescuers. They took their time arriving, believing that Farini's accident was simply part of the act.

The disappointing conclusion to his Niagara career did not stop Farini from a long and active life, which included oil painting, a stint as an explorer, and spying for the Union army during the American Civil War. He died in January 1929 at the age of 91 and was buried in Port Hope, Ontario.

Over the next few decades, several individuals tried to match the feats of Blondin and Farini. J.F. Jenkins crossed the gorge at the Whirlpool Rapids on a bicycle in August 25, 1869, but his performance was considered disappointing in comparison to Blondin's.

Four years later, Henry Bellini combined Blondin's tightrope-walking skills with Sam Patch's diving skills. The 32-year-old Australian walked along a tightrope until he was in the middle of the river, then jumped into the foaming water, where he was picked up by a waiting boat. Bellini repeated his stunt twice more in 1873. Thirteen years later, he tried diving from the Upper Suspension Bridge. He broke three ribs and was knocked out cold, but rescuers pulled him to safety and he recovered. Bellini's luck finally ran out in 1888, when he was killed jumping from a bridge in London, England.

An equally tragic fate befell Stephen Peer, who worked as Henry Bellini's assistant. Peer's job was to help put the ropes across the Niagara gorge. Peer had seen and admired Blondin's performances, and had tightrope walking ambitions of his own. Without the boss's permission, Peer used Bellini's ropes to cross the gorge. Bellini tried to stop him by cutting the tightrope, but was chased out of town by angry spectators.

Peer completed another walk the following year, then dropped out of sight for a time. By 1887 he was ready to try again. On June 22, walking on a 1.5-centimetre wire cable stretched between today's Whirlpool Bridge and the Penn Central Bridge, Peer crossed from the Canadian side, and back again. It had been 11 years since anyone had attempted a tightrope walk at Niagara, and for a time it seemed the glory days of Blondin had returned. But three nights later, after an evening of drinking, Peer tried the crossing in street shoes and plunged to his death.

When Queen Victoria Park commissioners assumed management of the reserve along the Niagara gorge on July 5, Peer's death was still fresh in everyone's mind. Tightrope walking across the gorge was promptly forbidden. Between Stephen Peer's second crossing and his last successful attempt, only one funambulist appeared at Niagara Falls. Maria Spelterini was the first — and only — woman to cross Niagara on a tightrope, as well as the first female daredevil at Niagara. She debuted on July 8, 1876, a buxom 23 year old of Italian descent whose physical charms drew almost as much attention as her aerial performance. Several newspaper reports wrote rapturously of the "superbly built" female funambulist in "flesh coloured tights, a tunic of scarlet, a sea-green bodice and neat green buskins."

Her first performance made crossing Niagara look as easy as a stroll in the park. Travelling on a 6-centimetre wire that one newspaper described as a "gossamer web," she stepped gracefully and confidently from the American side to the Canadian. For the trip back, she walked in time to waltz music provided by brass bands stationed on either shore.

Four days later she returned for an encore performance. This time, she had peach baskets strapped to her feet in place of her green boots. In subsequent performances, she crossed blindfolded, backwards, or with her hands and feet manacled.

After her final performance on July 16, 1876, she went to Buffalo and vanished almost as quickly as she had appeared. Nothing was ever heard of her again and the details of her personal life remain a mystery.

A number of tightrope walkers emerged after Stephen Peer's death, and, ignoring park regulations, made their own attempts to conquer Niagara. In

1870, Clifford Calverly, a 17-year-old steeplejack from Clarksburg, crossed the gorge at the unheard of speed of 2 minutes and 45 seconds. Most performers took between 10 to 15 minutes each way. Calverly made several more crossings, skipping rope, hanging by one arm, and using a wheelbarrow, but never achieved the fame of Blondin or Farini.

Others who followed included D.H. MacDonald, who made a successful crossing in 1887, and Charles Cromwell, the son of circus performers, who crossed twice, in 1887 and 1890. James E. Hardy made 16 crossings in 1896. Another man, a circus rope-walker named Oliver Hilton, claimed to have crossed the gorge on Hardy's rope in 1897, but was unable to prove it. On June 25, 1911, Oscar Williams tried to revive interest in tightrope walking, but the crowd that turned out was disappointingly small.

For more than 60 years, tightrope performers were a thing of the past. Then Henri Julien Rechatin arrived on the scene. Like Blondin, he was a Frenchman. The son of professional acrobats, Rechatin grew up in the circus world and eventually became a high-wire performer. In 1966, he set a world record for high-wire balancing, remaining on a cable 335 metres above the Loire Valley for 213 hours and 15 minutes.

The next year he was in Niagara Falls. With plans for Canada's centennial celebration underway, Rechatin made several proposals for high-wire acts across the Niagara River. The Niagara Parks Commission vetoed his proposals. He returned to France with his wife Janyck, but was back in May with another proposal. Again, authorities refused permission, and this time they threatened to prosecute if he attempted any stunts.

On June 3, 1975, Rechatin performed a chair-balancing act on the observation deck of the Skylon Tower. Atop a small wooden platform 160 metres above the ground, Rechatin placed one oak chair atop another, tipped it so that only two legs of the higher chair rested on the seat of the first, then climbed onto the upper chair and balanced on it for a few seconds. He repeated the trick three times during the day in order to draw attention to himself and his presence in Niagara Falls.

At 4:30 A.M. the following morning, Rechatin, Janyck and motorcyclist Frank Lucas of Toulouse, France gathered at the southern terminal of the Spanish Aerocar above the whirlpool. Two hours later, without official permission, Lucas drove his specially designed motorcycle onto the cable. Metal frames at the top and bottom of the cycle allowed

Rechatin to stand atop it while his wife dangled upside down below. They crossed most of the way on the cable, then Rechatin produced a balance pole and walked the remaining 5 metres to the northern terminal. After Janyck and Frank joined him there, Rechatin helped them into the Aerocar, where they waited until the operator arrived. When they reached the southern terminal, Rechatin was arrested for performing a dangerous act. Charges were later dropped.

In 1976, Rechatin, his wife, and daughter returned to Niagara Falls. This time, there was no attempt to cross Niagara Falls, although he did walk across wires strung between Ripley's Believe It or Not! Museum and the Hollywood Wax Museum in downtown Niagara Falls.

Henri Rechatin made subsequent proposals for stunts, but authorities turned him down. The day of the funambulist was officially over. At least it seemed that way, until October 1986.

Phillipe Pettit, a 25-year-old Frenchman, had visited Niagara in 1974 and tried to persuade officials to allow him to walk a high wire between Prospect Point Park on the American side and Table Rock, just above Horseshoe Falls. The Niagara Parks Commission turned him down. Pettit took his skills elsewhere, joining Ringling Brothers & Barnum and Bailey

Circus, and later walking a wire between New York's World Trade Centre towers at a height of 410 metres. In 1986 he returned to Niagara Falls. This time he walked a 15-metre cable 52 metres above Niagara.

The stunt was part of an IMAX movie, *Niagara: Miracle, Myths and Magic,* and Pettit's role was to recreate Blondin's high-wire act.

Chapter 3
Boats, Barrels, and Rafts

n the spring of 1861, *Maid of the Mist II* was sold to a Canadian company. In order to deliver the 22-metre steamer to her new owners, Captain Joel Robinson agreed to sail the boat through the rapids and whirlpool to Queenston, Ontario. In exchange, the crew would split a $500 reward.

The journey began at 3 P.M. Accompanied by mechanic James McIntyre and engineer James Jones, Robinson set out on the dangerous journey. Crowds of well-wishers thronged both sides of the river to see the sailors off.

Within a very short time, the boat was caught in the waves and tossed through the rocky waters. But the whirlpool was relatively calm, and Robinson managed to regain control. Then another problem emerged — the *Maid of the Mist* was caught in the vortex, and it was only with great difficulty that the ship broke free.

One more obstacle lay ahead — the Devil's Hole Rapids. Again, the waters beat at the *Maid of the Mist*, but Robinson and his crew fought back and finished the journey.

Although the boat lost a smokestack, Robinson completed his mission and delivered the *Maid of the Mist* to her new owners. But the adventure came at a high price for the 53-year-old captain. The frightening experience forced him into retirement, and he died two years later.

For skilled boatmen, the lower Niagara River presents a nearly insurmountable obstacle. Sensible sailors know better than to risk their lives in the roiling water. Yet, over the years, there have been dozens foolhardy enough to test their boating prowess in the rapids and the whirlpool. Miraculously, most have managed to survive.

Robert Flack was one of the unfortunate ones. On July 4, 1888, he drowned while crossing the

Whirlpool Rapids. Flack wagered his life on a boat filled with wood shavings to keep it afloat, and equipped with a number of harnesses to keep him from being tossed out of the vessel. He had not anticipated the boat would turn turtle. Unable to right the craft or free himself, Flack drowned in the waters of the whirlpool.

Two months later, Charles A. Percy made his second successful navigation of the Whirlpool Rapids. His first adventure took place on August 28, 1887, but a planned journey to Lewiston had to be called off when the boat became stuck in the whirlpool. Back for another attempt on September 16, 1888, he got through the whirlpool safely and continued through the Devil's Hole Rapids, before the rough water tossed him out of the boat. Fortunately, he was wearing a life preserver, and floated relatively unscathed down to Lewiston.

More than 10 years passed before another serious attempt was made to travel down the Niagara River. In July 1900, Peter "Bowser" Nissen arrived with a specially constructed boat. About 7 metres long, 2 metres wide, and a metre deep, it was almost completely covered. The centre cockpit, which was exposed, was equipped with several air compartments. At first, it seemed Nissen would complete his journey with little problem. Then the boat became caught in the whirlpool, and was trapped for an hour before Nissen was able to bring it to shore. Although he completed the journey the next day, he was not satisfied with the outcome, and over the winter months redesigned the vessel. On October 12, 1901, Nissen returned with a longer, narrower boat sporting a larger rudder, and more ballast to keep it afloat. This time, the trip was a success.

In 1910, the Niagara International Carnival Committee tried to lure visitors to the falls by promoting a boat race through the Whirlpool Rapids. Only one man responded — Captain Klaus Larsen. On September 18, 1910, Larsen covered the same route his predecessors had, although he was thrown out of the boat as he neared Queenston. He returned the following year to complete two uneventful trips through the Whirlpool Rapids and lower river.

Although boaters drew a certain amount of interest, their high success rate made them less of an attraction than other daredevils, especially after "stunters" started going over the falls. For years, few boaters challenged the rapids, but on June 28, 1974, 36-year-old Edward Friedland of Welland, rode a rubber dinghy through the rapids into the whirlpool, and promptly became stuck. He whirled around for three hours before a helicopter that normally carried tourists over the falls came to the rescue. In 1975, Jim Sarten, a stuntman working for Playboy Productions, decided to take the place of a dummy during the filming of a television movie. Both Canadian and American authorities had granted permission to film a stunt in which a dummy floated through the Whirlpool Rapids on a raft made from a few planks and empty oil drums. Sarten nearly drowned in the whirlpool, but survived. His employer was fined $75 for allowing him to attempt the stunt.

Two years later, Kenneth Lagergren and a friend took a kayak through the Whirlpool Rapids. When they returned safely to shore, Lagergren was arrested. The friend, identified only as Charles, escaped. In 1981, Lagergren and three colleagues, Chris Spelius, Don Wheedon, and Carrie Ashton returned to paddle their kayaks through the Whirlpool Rapids for a television show, *The American Sportsmen*. Because all four were professionals and kayaking was deemed a sport, the Niagara Sports Commission allowed them to proceed. Although one kayak turned over briefly, all four participants survived.

Compared to boaters, significantly more attention was lavished on barrel riders. Evidently there was something more appealing about this kind of craft, something rough and ready and a little more dangerous, even though barrel riders made elaborate preparations.

The first person to ride a barrel in the Niagara River was Carlisle D. Graham. He was a cooper, a maker of barrels, originally born in England, but living in Philadelphia before moving to Niagara Falls. His journey began at the Whirlpool Bridge around 4 P.M. on July 11, 1886. Equipped with air valves and weighted with ballast, the 2-metre-long barrel was towed into the river and set adrift. "The barrel, with its human freight, was tossed about like a cork on the angry breakers, and shot the rapids with lightning speed," reported the *Globe* the next day. The trip through the rapids and the whirlpool took a total of nine minutes. Graham came ashore at Queenston unscathed, although he felt ill, possibly from lack of oxygen or from being tossed around in the barrel. When he drove back to Niagara Falls, he announced that he would make additional trips. The following morning he was arrested. "He expressed himself very tired and his nerves very much unstrung," the Toronto newspaper noted. "He felt himself badly shaken up pounding over the rocks, going through the rapids."

Graham recovered quickly and, despite official

Carlisle Graham, the first to go through the Whirlpool Rapids in a barrel attempts to prevent a repetition of the stunt, announced he would make his second trip on August 19, this time with his head outside the barrel. Before the day arrived, two acquaintances decided to steal his thunder. On August 8, George Hazlett and William Potts went into a barrel together and became the first pair to travel through the rapids. Undeterred, Graham made the second trip as scheduled, keeping his head outside the barrel. Again he survived, but suffered hearing loss as a result.

While Graham seemed to revel in the attention, he was willing to share the limelight with others. In November 1886, for example, he loaned his barrel to George Hazlett and Sadie Allen, who became the first male/female daredevil team to challenge the rapids at Niagara.

On June 15, 1887, the *Memphis Avalanche* reported that Carlisle Graham would repeat his performance of taking a barrel through the Whirlpool Rapids that afternoon, "but instead of being inside, he will be strapped by his feet and hands to the outside of the barrel." He survived that adventure, and on August 25, 1889, made a fourth trip. By this time Graham was being hailed as the "Hero of Niagara," greatly admired for his daring and his outstanding string of good luck. But after his fourth ride through the rapids, he rashly announced he would go over the falls in a barrel. He sent an empty barrel over the waterfall as a test, but did not make the trip himself. Although there was absolutely no evidence of a barrel ride over the falls, Graham claimed he had done just that. No one believed him, and his brief popularity faded.

Still, he had one final brief fling with fame. On July 17, 1905, Graham and William J. Glover of Baltimore staged a race through the Devil's Hole Rapids. Glover won the race, a $200 prize, and probably part of a $1000 side bet. Graham was in his mid-40s at the time, still in excellent physical shape but no match for the much younger Glover. Following the race, the "Hero of Niagara" faded into obscurity.

Yet even as his fame was waning, Graham's barrel continued to test the waters of Niagara. On September 6, 1901, Martha E. Wagenfuhrer borrowed it. Wife of a professional wrestler, Martha was born in Germany, but had been living in Buffalo for some time. After several drinks one afternoon, Martha climbed into the barrel and was towed away shortly before 6 P.M. that evening. The barrel headed directly for the whirlpool, where it stayed for several hours.

While Martha's friends contacted authorities and arranged for a searchlight to be focussed on the whirlpool, others managed to catch the barrel and tow it to the Canadian side. Martha had to be helped out. One report suggested she was seasick after her time spinning in the whirlpool, but another newspaper pointed to the amount of liquor she had consumed prior to her stunt. "It is highly probable that she did not know anything about the trip." Whether or not she was fully aware of her journey, Martha went on to thrill audiences in vaudeville theatres with stories about her barrel ride.

Meanwhile, a dynasty of Niagara daredevils was being established. In 1888, two years after Carlisle Graham's first barrel ride, William "Red" Hill was born in Niagara Falls. On May 30, 1930, Red Hill Sr. rode in a barrel from the *Maid of the Mist* landing, just downstream of the Horseshoe Falls, to Queenston. The steel barrel was a metre around and 2 metres long, but only 1.5 metres long inside because of bulkheads installed in either end. Air holes along the sides were plugged with corks to keep the water out, but could be opened in an emergency. Like Graham, Red was concerned about being tossed around during his journey, so he installed a harness system that kept him away from the walls. Outside, the barrel proclaimed in red and gold letters, "William Red Hill, Master Hero of Niagara."

Niagara Daredevils

No one doubted his bravery. After English stunt-man Bobby Leach rode a barrel through the rapids in 1910, Red helped pull Leach and the barrel to shore. Someone bet Red $2 to ride the barrel down the river. Without hesitation, he jumped in it and floated off to Queenston.

Red was a river man with an encyclopedic knowledge of the behaviour of the currents, under-tows, and whirlpools. He learned of the river's power first-hand as a five year old when his father, Layfield, swam into the river with the boy on his back. A keen observer of the water and the weather that affected it, he spent hours throwing sticks, cans, and other objects into the river and predicting where they would come ashore. That insight came in handy whenever a drowning victim had to be recovered — Red recovered a total of 177 bodies from the river during his lifetime.

The bodies gave Red a profound appreciation of the river's dangers. But he also knew it was possible to beat the odds. On numerous occasions, he had saved people from its waters. One of the most spectacular rescues took place during the "Ice Bridge Disaster."

At the beginning of the 20th century, the Niagara River usually froze solid. Many tourists came to experience Niagara in winter. People wandered along the "ice bridge" formed by frozen waters below the falls, sometimes building shacks for ice fishing.

Red Hill was in one of the shacks on the late morning of February 4, 1912. Unbeknownst to him, his companions, or the groups out on the ice, shifting winds had loosened the ice. Sitting in the shack Red sensed the ice shifting and hurried to shore. But when he spotted a group of tourists paralyzed with fear, he rushed back to escort them to safety.

Three people died that day: a honeymooning couple from Toronto — Mr. and Mrs. Eldridge Stanton — and 18-year-old Burrell Peacock of Cleveland, who Red tried to rescue. The ice on which the trio was standing broke loose and floated downstream, tossing them all into the frigid rapids.

As a soldier in World War I, Red Hill was wounded twice and severely injured in a gas attack. Yet barely days after he returned from the war, he was involved in another rescue. This time a river scow had broken loose, and two men were stranded in the river just above Horseshoe Falls. A breeches buoy sent out to carry the pair to safety was caught in the current, becoming so entangled with ropes holding the scow in place that it was rendered useless. Red waded into the rushing waters to free it, and the men were saved.

By 1930, Red had seen a variety of daredevils come and go. Some of their stunts succeeded, others proved fatal. Although many of the daredevils had set out to gain fame and fortune, none really succeeded. Yet Red Hill finally succumbed to the call of Niagara. On May 30, 1930, he climbed into a barrel of his own.

"Niagara Conquered by Daring Riverman Encased in Barrel" blared the front page headlines of the *Toronto Globe*. It was a hard battle. Red set out just before 1:30 P.M. and spent more than 90 minutes caught in the current. Then the barrel reached the whirlpool, where it whirled round and round for three and a half hours. Finally, with the help of some friends, the barrel was pulled free and continued on to Queenston. When it arrived at 6:15 P.M. Red Jr. rowed out to meet his father, who emerged bruised and battered, but triumphant. Waiting on the dock was Red's wife, Beatrice, with their seven other children, including a 16-day-old baby.

The next year he tried the same stunt, but this time used the barrel in which Greek cook George Stathakis had plunged to his death over the falls. Once again, the barrel was caught in the whirlpool, causing Red Jr. to mutter about a jinx. In fact, the barrel was taking on water, and by the time it reached the whirlpool, it was half full. With a rope tied around his waist, Red Jr. jumped into the water and swam to the barrel. He tied the rope to it, attempting to pull it back to shore, but it took the combined strength of 12 men to pull Red Hill Sr. to safety.

The river won that round, but Red Sr. was not about to admit defeat. The following day, without telling anyone, he climbed back into the barrel and rode the rest of the way to Queenston.

Red Hill Sr. died of a heart attack in May 1942. Three years later, 19-year-old Red Jr. assumed his father's unofficial throne as king of the Niagara River. His plan was to carry out a stunt to raise money for a suitable memorial to Red Hill Sr.

Parks Commission officials got wind of the stunt sometime beforehand, and kept a close eye on the teen. They assumed he would launch his 720-pound barrel from the *Maid of the Mist* docks, but Red Jr. had other plans. The barrel — the same one his father had used in 1931 — was quietly removed from the family's souvenir shop and hidden on the Canadian side, just south of the Whirlpool Rapids. At 1 P.M. he changed into old clothes and slipped into the barrel.

It was a rough ride. Just before reaching the rapids, a wave struck the barrel sideways, tossing it more than 6 metres into the air. It tipped end over end twice before slamming back into the water.

Major (his given name) and Norman Hill, Red's brothers, rowed out and brought the barrel to shore. Red Jr. emerged briefly, complaining of dizziness, but gamely climbed back into the barrel and continued his journey.

At 4.22 P.M., the barrel passed under the Lewiston Bridge. A motorboat, the *Patsy Jean* chugged out to meet it. Red Jr., who had already popped his head out of the barrel, grabbed the line tossed by a friend and was pulled to the dock where hundreds waited to congratulate him.

The Hills' souvenir shop did a bustling business that day, and collected quite a bit of money for Red Sr.'s memorial. But the excitement took its toll on Beatrice, who suffered a heart attack that evening.

She recovered, and so did Red. But there was no remedy for his obsession with Niagara. One September 6, 1948, still claiming he needed money for his father's memorial fund, he took a second barrel ride. Although he used a larger barrel, the journey was remarkably similar — first thrown into the air by waves and then caught in the whirlpool for more than an hour until one of Red's brothers pulled it free. Red Jr. completed the journey to the Queenston dock in four and a half hours, but the fortune he sought continued to elude him. A few weeks later, creditors forced the sale of all Hill family possessions, including three barrels that had been used in Niagara River rides. Lack of money, a need to uphold the family's reputation, and perhaps a desire to outdo his legendary father eventually led Red Jr. to a fateful decision. On August 5, 1951, he would go over the falls. This time, rather than use a barrel, he would ride *The Thing*, an awkward cigar-like concoction of 13 heavy duty inner tubes held together by canvas webbing and wrapped in chunky fish netting.

An estimated 150,000 people were watching Horseshoe Falls shortly before 3 P.M., as Red Jr. was towed into the upper river and cut loose near Navy Island. At 3:03, *The Thing* was swept over the falls and smashed into fragments. Red vanished, and rumours circulated that he had not gone over the falls at all. Unfortunately, the rumours were false. Red's battered body turned up at the *Maid of the Mist* dock the following day.

Meanwhile, his younger brother vowed to continue the family tradition. Although he was still a private in the Canadian army, Major Hill announced he would go over the falls on August 13th, just eight days after his brother's death. His mother apparently talked him out of it, although he subsequently made four barrel rides through the rapids, in 1949, 1950,

1954, and 1956. In spite of the family's fame, Major lacked the charisma his father and older brother had possessed, and never attracted the same attention. He committed suicide in 1974.

By the 1970s, Carlisle Graham and the Hill family had faded into legend. Meanwhile, adventure travel was becoming popular. Knowing that individuals far less skilled than Graham or the Hills would pay for the thrill of running the rapids, a Toronto promoter established Niagara Gorge Trips Inc.

Whitewater rafting was becoming popular in many places, and despite occasional mishaps seemed relatively safe. Although another company's 1972 attempt to establish regular raft trips had failed, Niagara Gorge Trips Inc. put its confidence in a specially designed 10-metre rubber Zodiac raft. Starting in early August 1975, members of the media, company employees, and others were invited to participate in a series of trial runs. On August 29, 1975, the raft flipped, dumping 27 passengers and two crew members into the raging water. Despite valiant rescue efforts, three people died when they were trapped beneath the overturned raft.

Wesley Hill, last surviving son of Red Hill Sr., was among the rescuers. His comments to reporters summed up the dangers looming in the lower

Boats, Barrels, and Rafts

Niagara River, "Rapids are never the same on any two days. A current can hit you unexpectedly anywhere. It's impossible to figure out any safe path through."

Chapter 4
Accidental Daredevils

**O**ver the years, dozens of people have challenged Niagara Falls in a deliberate attempt to achieve fame or gain riches. But some individuals, both human and animal, have conquered Niagara entirely by accident. One of the first was the legendary Maid of the Mist.

While some claim that the story of the Maid of the Mist is based on native legend, in all likelihood, the story was a romantic tale concocted by Victorian tourism promoters. During the 19th century, one popular version was written by Rosanna Eleanor Leprohon, a Montreal writer who published her

Poetical Works in 1881. Set out in verse was the story of "The White Canoe."

In Leprohon's version, Native peoples gathered once a year to offer a human sacrifice to the spirit of the falls. Traditionally, this sacrifice was a white canoe brimming with fruits and flowers, which was paddled over the cataract by the fairest girl of the tribe. Although it was considered a great honour to be chosen, when Minahita, daughter of Chief Tolonga was selected, her father was grief-stricken. On the fateful night, Minahita calmly paddled her canoe towards the roaring falls. At the very last moment Tolonga leaped into his own birchbark, paddled furiously out to meet her, and together father and daughter plunged over the falls.

Another version of the legend tells of Lelawala, daughter of Chief Eagle Eye, who was chosen to appease the Thunder God, who lived in a cave behind the falls. Like Minahita, Lelawala paddled a white canoe filled with flowers and fruit over the falls, and her broken-hearted father followed her. But this time, the sons of Hinum, the Thunder God, fell in love with the girl, and rescued her. When both proposed marriage, Lelawala promised to wed the man who would tell her why so many of her people were dying. The younger brother explained that a great water snake lived at the foot of the falls. Once a year it became hungry, poisoned the village water supply, and then consumed those who died.

Lelawala visited her people in spirit form and warned them about the snake. The warriors attacked it, and the dying snake returned to its den, where its body formed the semi-circle that became Horseshoe Falls. Lelawala returned to live in the cave of the Thunder God, although it was said that at certain times she could be seen in the mist of the falls.

In the legends, the Maid of the Mist was caught up in circumstances beyond her control. A similar lack of choice caused the death of a boatload of animals in the earliest and cruellest publicity stunt at Niagara Falls. In 1827, three hotel owners, William Forsyth, John Brown, and General Parkhurst Whitney, teamed up to bring crowds to Niagara. Forsyth, an ex-smuggler and owner of the Pavilion Hotel, bought a condemned 5-metre schooner, *Michigan.* The three men then dreamed up a scheme in which the *Michigan* would be rigged up like a pirate ship with effigies of crewmembers stationed around the vessel. Also aboard would be imprisoned passengers, "Animals of the most ferocious kind, such as Panthers, Wild cats, Bears, and Wolves" if they could be captured from the surrounding forests, as well as "a few vicious or worthless dogs" and "a few of the toughest of the Lesser Animals."

According to the publicity surrounding the event, Captain James Rough of Black Rock, New York, assisted by Levi Allen, would arrange the voyage, which would start on the morning of September 8. The *Michigan* would be towed from Black Rock to Navy Island, and then out into the river.

It was expected that if the *Michigan* steered through the deepest water of the river, she had a good chance of surviving the drop down the falls intact. As for the animals, if they were "young and hardy and possessed of great muscular powers," they also had a chance of survival. Those who lived would be rounded up and sent for exhibit to museums in New York, Montreal, and London.

Thousands of people turned out to witness what turned into a gala event complete with gamblers, vendors, and refreshment booths. At 3 P.M. as planned, the *Michigan* was towed out.

The event hardly lived up to its billing. The menagerie consisted of a pitiful assembly of two small bears, a buffalo, two foxes, an eagle, a racoon, a dog, and 15 geese. Contrary to predictions, the *Michigan* did not survive the journey. Well before it approached the brink of the falls, she began to fall apart and the bears and the buffalo jumped ship. The bears swam to Goat Island, where one was later caught and put on display. Meanwhile, the derelict steamer lost her masts, and broke in half before she reached the falls. The trip over completed the destruction, and all of the remaining animals died except a lone goose.

Despite a growing sentimentality towards them, during the Victorian period there were few laws that protected animals from human cruelty. As a result, some daredevils thought nothing of involving their pets in stunts. Sam Patch threw his pet bear into the river on at least one occasion before taking the plunge himself. Before Anna Edson Taylor attempted her 1901 barrel ride, she and an associate placed a cat in a barrel and sent it over the falls. The cat survived, encouraging Taylor to proceed with her stunt.

Another daredevil, Walter Campbell brought his dog, Jumbo, along on a wild ride through the Whirlpool Rapids on September 15, 1888. Campbell was just a few weeks short of his 20th birthday when he and some friends set out along the Niagara River in a clinker-built boat. At the old *Maid of the Mist* landing, he dropped off his friends, then, wearing bathing trunks and a cork life preserver, rowed away from shore with the intention of riding the boat through the Whirlpool Rapids.

As the boat reached the churning water, Jumbo was thrown out. Moments later, Campbell lost an oar. On shore, spectators saw him clutch either side of the small boat. Pounded by waves, the small craft began taking on water and broke up. Campbell was tossed into the rapids, where he had to fight against the strength of the current while dodging bits of debris. Somehow he made it to the Canadian shore, where he was hailed as a hero. Jumbo was not so lucky. The dog drowned after it was flung out of the boat.

Another dog was more fortunate. On September 7, 1901, Carlisle D. Graham and Maude Willard staged a two-person stunt. Only a day earlier, Martha Wagenfuhrer had become the first woman to ride solo through the rapids and whirlpool. Graham, already a noted daredevil, persuaded Maude to duplicate the feat, with an added twist. When the barrel she was riding in came out of the rapids and headed for Lewiston, New York, Graham would swim alongside.

Maude, a burlesque performer from Canton, Ohio insisted on bringing along her pet fox terrier. At 3:40 P.M., she climbed into the barrel. About 15 minutes later, Graham rowed a small boat into the middle of the river, towing the barrel behind. By four, the barrel had passed the lower suspension bridge. Five minutes more brought it into the whirlpool. But instead of moving through it and onto the American shore, the barrel was caught in the vortex. It remained upright, but spun round and round until people grew tired of watching.

Meanwhile, because a movie cameraman had been brought in, Graham was forced to complete his swim on to Lewiston. Buoyed by a life preserver and a flotation ring around his head, he completed the journey, and returned to the whirlpool, where the barrel continued to bob in the water. There had been just one slight change, according to eyewitnesses. Around 5 o'clock, the barrel had disappeared suddenly. When it resurfaced, it listed to one side. There was speculation that Maude had lost consciousness and slumped over inside.

Graham swam out to try to bring the barrel in, but was unable to reach it. As the light failed, searchlights were trained on the spinning barrel. A second man, Captain Billy Johnson, used long ropes and life preservers, but also failed to rescue Maude. Finally Archibald Donald, a young man who had recently saved someone from drowning in the whirlpool, swam out and managed to tow the barrel into calmer waters. By this time it was after midnight, and a number of Maude's friends had gathered on shore. But there would be no happy reunion. When the barrel was opened, rescuers found Maude dead.

According to a report in the *Hamilton Evening Times*, many of Maude's friends were drunk, and stumbled and swore by the light of torches as they "half carried, half dragged the body of the woman by her feet and hair of her head." The consensus was that Maude had suffocated when the fox terrier's muzzle became stuck in the air hole of the barrel.

With Martha Wagenfuhrer's success fresh in her memory, Maude Willard probably expected the barrel ride would be a lark, and wanted her dog to share the glory. But another daredevil brought along an animal companion as insurance in case of his own death.

A self-styled mystic, who believed he had been born in Central Africa a millennium earlier, George Stathakis was a 46-year-old short-order cook in Buffalo. Born in Greece, he had developed a complex philosophy before emigrating to the U.S., and had written a number of books on the subject. He was fascinated by Niagara, frequently going out in a boat and edging nearer and nearer to the roaring water of the falls.

Jean Lussier's successful plunge over the falls in

1928 inspired George to prepare for a similar trip. He wanted fame, but not from the stunt. What he really wanted was $5000 to finance the publication of a three-volume series tracing the history of mankind from ancient times and predicting the future.

Although acquaintances, notably riverman Red Hill Sr., tried to talk him out of it, Stathakis built a huge wooden barrel, 3 metres long, 1.5 metres around and reinforced with steel at both ends. A number of bolts would secure the lid in place.

At 3:35 on the afternoon of July 5, 1930, George set out on his adventure over the falls. With him he took a turtle, Sonny Boy, who was reputedly 105 years old. According to Stathakis, Sonny Boy possessed his own kind of wisdom. "If I die, the turtle will carry the secret of the trip and reveal it at the proper time."

George was dapperly dressed, his full moustache neatly arranged as he was helped into the barrel. A mattress was stuffed inside, along with an air tank. The barrel was cut loose near Navy Island and went over the falls with little problem. But, unlike any other barrel before or since, it became trapped behind the water. There it stayed for 14 hours, long after George's air supply had run out. When the barrel finally emerged at dawn on the morning of July 6, Red Hill Sr. hauled it to shore. It took several more hours for him to break through the bolts that Stathakis had fastened into place. Inside, he found George's body, tightly strapped to a sodden mattress. According to the *Toronto Daily Star*, he was still clutching a pad and pencil that he brought along in hopes of jotting down his impressions of the ride.

Also inside was Sonny Boy, who had survived. Red Hill displayed the turtle in a tent near his taxi stand on the grounds of Lafayette Hotel, charging tourists a small fee to look at it, as well as Stathakis's barrel. When a Buffalo couple kidnapped Sonny Boy, Hill chased them in his own taxi. After he lost them, he hired a detective to find the turtle, which was eventually returned and put back on display. However, if he had gained any knowledge on George's final journey, Sonny Boy kept it to himself. Despite his owner's predictions, the turtle never reported on what they had experienced behind the veil of Horseshoe Falls.

And for that matter, the veil of secrecy surrounding the personal life of George Stathakis was never lifted either. No one ever claimed his body.

Of all the individuals who went over Niagara Falls and lived to tell about it, no one can claim a more life-altering experience than Roger Woodward. His adventure started on July 9, 1960, when a friend of his father stopped by the Woodward family trailer.

Jim Honeycutt was a foreman at the Moses power plant in Niagara Falls, New York. A native of North Carolina, he was a strong swimmer and an experienced boater who loved the water. On July 9, 1960, he asked co-worker Frank Woodward if he and his family would like to take a ride in his boat.

Woodward and his wife declined, but gave Deanne, 17, and Roger, 7, permission to accompany Honeycutt. It was extremely hot and Roger was uncomfortable with his life jacket on. But the boy was only learning to swim and before he left the house his father made him promise to wear his life jacket for the duration of the boat trip. When Roger complained about the heat in the boat, Honeycutt reminded him of that promise.

Honeycutt wanted to give the youngsters a good view of the rapids, and took the boat out beyond the Grand Island Bridge, into the turbulent waters that cautious boaters avoided. He also allowed Roger to steer the boat for a while. It was a pleasant ride, and an exciting one for the children.

Then there was a loud noise, and excitement swiftly turned to terror.

The boat's propeller was damaged on a shoal. Without a motor, the 4-metre aluminum craft was powerless against the swift current. As Honeycutt grabbed the oars and rowed frantically upstream, he called to Deanne to put on a life jacket — the only other one aboard.

Seconds later, a tremendous wave hit the boat. Somehow, it remained upright. Then another wave hit, and the boat flipped end over end. Deanne held on for a few moments, until the current swept her towards Goat Island. Two men were standing on the shore. One was John Hayes, a truck driver from New Jersey who was visiting Terrapin Point. He climbed a guard-rail, reached out and grabbed Deanne's fingers. Deanne was just 5 metres from the brink of the falls, and Hayes was not sure how much longer he could hold on. Then John Quattrochi, a 39-year-old tourist from Pennsgrove, New Jersey, came running. He grabbed Deanne's thumb and helped pull her to safety.

"My brother," she cried. "What's happened to my brother?"

Hayes and others had already seen Honeycutt and the boy swept over Horseshoe Falls. Unwilling to break the news to the shaken girl, Quattrochi suggested Deanne pray for Roger.

While Deanne was being swept towards Goat Island, Jim Honeycutt held a panic-stricken Roger in his arms until they neared the brink, and the force of the water pushed them apart. Roger felt every rock in the water as he hurtled towards the edge. His running shoes were torn from his feet, and then it seemed he was flying. But he was lucky. He weighed only 55 pounds, and because of his small size the water threw him in a wide arc away from the rocky precipice behind the falls. Although he plunged into the deep water at the bottom of the falls, he quickly rose to the surface.

It was 12:55. *Maid of the Mist* was making its regular trip, approaching the base of the falls so tourists could get a better look. To the amazement of Captain Clifford Keech and his passengers, an orange life jacket suddenly appeared. Almost instantly, the tourists realized the jacket was keeping a young boy afloat. Roger was about 90 metres from the falls, nearly beyond the reach of rescuers.

Captain Keech edged the *Maid of the Mist* as close to the falls as he could, while a crewman tossed a life preserver to Roger. He was too far away. A second attempt also failed. On the third try, Roger was able to grab hold of the life preserver. He flopped onto the lifebuoy, and immediately asked about his sister.

Roger was cut and bruised, but otherwise safe. John Quattrochi, who had witnessed Roger's rescue from the observation point atop the falls, relayed the good news to Deanne.

Jim Honeycutt's body was found four days later. Roger was taken to hospital in Niagara Falls, Ontario, where he was treated for minor injuries. He recalled every moment of his ordeal for reporters — the panic, the struggle with the water, wanting to see his sister and parents again, and finally the rescue. However, he was apparently too young to fully appreciate how miraculous his experience had been, even with all the media attention that surrounded his dramatic rescue.

Jean Lussier, a daredevil who had gone over the falls and survived, watched Roger's rescue from a distance. Contacted by reporters, he said, "The Lord was with the boy. It just wasn't his time to die." That was a sentiment Roger himself would eventually express. Although Deanne preferred not to relive her horrifying experience, his brush with death haunted Roger for many years. Eventually he turned to religion, convinced that he had been saved for a greater purpose, to bring the word of God to others. Thirty years after his fateful journey, he returned to Niagara Falls to preach in Glendale Alliance Church.

Chapter 5
Over the Falls

t was a new century and a new world. Queen Victoria, who had ruled since 1837, had died peacefully in January. Women had made great strides forward, winning the right to vote in some municipal elections, as well as the right to higher education and entry into previously all-male professions. At Niagara Falls, a century that had seen a parade of daredevils swim the rapids, ride in boats and barrels and jump off bridges gave way to an era where the focus of risk-takers became the falls themselves. The height of the American Falls and the huge pile of rocks below them made them

too dangerous for daredevils, but the Horseshoe Falls presented risk-takers with a more manageable challenge. Going over the Horseshoe Falls would become the obsession of 20th century daredevils. And leading the way was a woman.

Although she portrayed herself as a respectable, conventional widow, Anna Edson Taylor was exceptional in many ways. She had earned her own living for much of her life, ever since her doctor husband died while she was still in her late teens. She had wandered all over North America, visited Cuba and Europe, but never quite settled down. In 1901 she was 63, although she claimed to be 20 years younger, and she was desperate to make a name for herself and enough money to keep her comfortable in her old age.

After reading about Carlisle Graham's fifth trip through the Whirlpool Rapids on July 15, 1901, Annie decided she would become a Niagara daredevil. She would beat the men at their own game, riding a barrel over the falls. There was a risk, of course, but as far as Annie was concerned, death was no worse than living off the charity of relatives. She travelled to Niagara Falls, New York and began making arrangements.

One of the most important preparations was the construction of a barrel. She hired a Niagara Falls cooper, John Rozenski, to build a sturdy container of

Anna, wearing a large hat, en route to Grass Island

white Kentucky oak. Measuring 56 centimetres around at the top, 86 centimetres in the middle, and 38 centimetres at the bottom, the barrel was 1.5 metres long and weighed 160 pounds. Inside was a 100-pound iron anvil, which was supposed to keep the barrel upright in the water.

Although the stunt was originally scheduled for October 20, it was postponed twice. Acquaintances tried to talk Annie out of the barrel ride, but she was adamant. She wanted fame and the fortune she was sure a successful ride over the falls would bring. Yet, at the same time, she tried to portray herself as a cut above the usual Niagara Falls daredevil. She disliked roistering, hard-drinking rivermen such as Carlisle Graham and Bobby Leach, and had nothing but disdain for women performers such as Maud Willard. Under no circumstances would she appear in the abbreviated costumes worn by the likes of Maria Spelterini or Martha Wagenfuhrer. On the day of her trip over Niagara, she wore a long black dress with lacy cuffs and a large black hat, an outfit that would have been completely acceptable at church. "I think it unbecoming a woman of refinement and of my years to parade before a crowd in a short skirt," she told reporters.

Still, long skirts and large hats were hardly appropriate for the confines of a wooden barrel. After she was rowed to Grass Island by rivermen Fred Truesdale and William Holloran, she hid behind some bushes, removed the hat, and changed into a shorter skirt and blouse. Then, with the assistance of Truesdale and Holloran, she climbed into the barrel, crouched down as the lid was nailed in place, and was towed out to the middle of the river.

At 4.05 P.M., the barrel was cut loose. All around the falls, people watched breathlessly, many of them turning pale as the barrel and its passenger approached the edge. Others bet that Mrs. Taylor would be dead before the barrel reached the falls. One reporter described what happened next:

The barrel glided gracefully over the brink about 20 feet towards the Canadian shore from the centre, where there is a deflection in the horseshoe, and shot down the awful plunge of 158 feet behind the mighty cloud of mist, disappearing for about two minutes. The crowd of spectators held its breath, but a mighty cheer went up when the black speck once more showed up from out of the mist cloud, serenely bobbing about in the white threshed waters at the base of the falls.

The barrel had survived the first test, dropping from the upper river intact. Almost as soon as it hit the lower river, it was caught in an eddy and swept towards the Canadian shore.

Four men hurried to intercept it. At 4:40 P.M., they grabbed hold of the barrel, pulled it out of the water and ripped off the cover. Inside, they found Annie, stunned, bleeding, disoriented, but still alive.

One of the men waved to the crowd, signalling that Mrs. Taylor had survived. But she was so dazed that she could not climb out of the barrel. Instead, the staves were sawed off so that she could be lifted out. "Nobody ought ever do that again," she commented. As blood dripped onto her jacket from a scalp wound, she was assisted into a boat, rowed to the *Maid of the Mist* landing, and taken to her boarding house.

A doctor was called to tend to her wounds. Although bruised, bleeding, and in shock, Annie was otherwise uninjured, and the doctor predicted she would make a full recovery. Meanwhile, the reporters began to gather, eager to hear Annie's version of the stupendous journey. They found her somewhat befuddled. "I was whirled around at lightning speed, and then I crashed into the rocks three times — oh, my head, my head," she said to the reporter of the *Mail and Empire*.

Newspapers hailed her as a heroine. Annie dubbed herself "Queen of the Mist" and was booked for a handful of public appearances, although much of the money she earned in the first few weeks was used to cover the expenses of her barrel ride. Unfortunately, her notions of respectability made her turn down some of the more lucrative offers at popular museums. And, lacking Martha Wagenfuhrer's common touch, she bombed as a guest speaker. Although she made a number of appearances in store windows with her barrel and a black cat — reputedly the same one that had been sent over the falls in a trial run — and wrote an autobiography, the fortune she had risked so much to gain never materialized. She became a pathetic figure, an elderly woman who dwelled on the memories of her brief shining moment of fame. In February 1921, she was admitted to the county poorhouse in Niagara Falls, New York. She died there in poverty two months later.

For nearly 10 years, Annie Taylor's feat was unrivalled. No one else attempted it.

Then Bobby Leach decided to add a trip over the falls to his repertoire of stunts. A circus performer originally from Cornwall, England, Leach was born in 1864. Unlike the respectable Mrs. Taylor, he fit right in with the rivermen who often assisted daredevils. A hard-drinking tavern owner, he usually had a cigar stuck in his mouth and often flaunted a diamond stickpin. He had successfully ridden the rapids in a barrel twice in June 1898. Ten years later, he parachuted off the Suspension Bridge. Finally, on July 25, 1911, while a movie camera whirred, he attempted the third part of the "triple crown" of Niagara stunting.

The announcement that he would make the attempt came at 1 P.M. on July 25. The barrel he chose for the ride was made of sturdy steel, 2.5 metres long

Bobby Leach in his barrel, 1911

and shaped like a cigar. Bobby and his buddies knew enough about the river to predict where the barrel was likely to land, and several men were stationed on the rocks near the Ontario Hydro station, ropes at the ready.

After a lengthy delay, Bobby, who had been drinking heavily, swaggered onto the scene, climbed into the barrel, and was towed into the river. He tumbled around in the barrel as it moved swiftly downstream. Then, at 3:12 P.M. the barrel dropped over the falls.

Once again, Niagara's changeable nature revealed itself. Rather than moving towards the waiting rescuers, it swept past them and out of reach of their ropes. Thinking quickly, Frank Bender, an employee with Ontario Hydro, called for a rope, tied it under his armpits and jumped into the water fully dressed.

Had brash Bobby Leach finally met his match? The crowd waited anxiously as the barrel was pulled onto land. Harris Williams rapped on it with a hammer. Immediately, there was an answering tap from inside and the rescuers cheered. A few moments later, the manhole-like cover was removed and Bobby was hauled out.

Leach had sustained serious injuries, including a broken jaw and shattered kneecaps, but he was in great spirits. "Somebody send to my wife and tell her I'm all right," he requested as soon as he was pulled out of the barrel. After a few minutes, he commented, "I feel better now, and if someone will just give me a cigar, I'll be all right."

After recuperating from his injuries for several weeks in hospital, he went on tour. Although he never again attempted a trip over the falls, on July 1, 1920 and again on October 10, 1925, he parachuted out of a plane, but rather than landing in the Niagara River as planned, he dropped into Canadian cornfields.

Although he was in his 60s by this time, he again lived to tell the tale.

But Bobby Leach's life ended on an ironic note. During a visit to New Zealand with his daughter, he slipped on an orange peel while out on his daily walk, fell, and broke his leg. Gangrene set in and he died in April 1926, half a world away from the falls that had fascinated him. As a long-time fixture at Niagara Falls, Bobby Leach had seen many daredevils come and go. Sometimes, he provided them with advice, although they did not necessarily heed it. Such was the case with Charles Stephens, who tried to duplicate Bobby's feat on July 11, 1920.

Like Leach, Stephens was an Englishman, a Bristol barber with a family of 11 children. He already had a reputation as a stuntman in his native land, having made a number of high dives. Although his wife, Annie, tried to talk him out of it, the 58-year-old Stephens was determined to go over the falls. He hired a Toronto motion picture crew to film the event, planning to show the movie at concert halls in England.

Stephens's barrel was made of thick Russian oak, held together by steel hoops. An anvil was placed in the bottom to keep the barrel upright, and there were straps inside in which Stephens could place his arms. Bobby Leach and Red Hill Sr. were both aware of

Stephens's preparations, although Leach tried to persuade his fellow countryman not to risk his life. Stephens refused to listen, viewing Leach's advice as a tactic to preserve his reputation as the only man to make the trip over the falls. He also refused Red Hill's suggestion to test the barrel by sending it over the falls empty.

The experiences of Annie Taylor and Bobby Leach should have made it clear that anyone who rode over the falls in a barrel would be tossed around during the journey. Even with pillows stuffed into the barrel, Taylor had been bruised and cut. But Charles Stephens was something of a fatalist. He wore padded clothing, but took no other precautions. And a great deal of persuasion was needed to convince him to take a tank of air along.

Once he had made up his mind to go over the falls, Stephens proceeded calmly. To escape detection by Park Commission authorities, he checked into a hotel under an assumed name. He prepared two telegrams — one announcing his success, the other announcing his death — and left instructions to send whichever was appropriate. Late on the night of Saturday, July 10, he left the barrel near Snyder's Point, about 5 kilometres upstream of the falls.

After rising early on the morning of July 11, he

quietly made his way to the barrel. He appeared "perfectly at ease" according to eyewitnesses. "He had absolute confidence in his barrel and in the oxygen supply outfit, which he was testing out for the inventor, with a view to having the device ultimately used by divers."

As it turned out, his confidence in the barrel was hopelessly misplaced. Ninety metres from shore one of the hoops broke off. One of the fellows helping Stephens examined it, and the decision was made to continue.

Past Navy Island, the barrel was cut loose. It rapidly picked up speed, hurtling towards the falls. And then it disappeared. Spectators waited. Ten minutes passed, then 20, and there was still no sign. In the interim, a *Globe* reporter questioned Bobby Leach. "Has he any chance?" he asked the Niagara daredevil.

"No chance," Leach replied. "I told him yesterday that his barrel wasn't strong enough. The hoops were too light. The hoops on my barrel were bent, and they were twice as thick."

For three hours, spectators and Stephens's colleagues waited. Finally, around noon, a stave broke loose and bobbed to the surface. More wreckage appeared over the next few hours. Apparently when the barrel hit the water the anvil went through the bottom, shattering the container. After searching all night, rescuers found no trace of Stephens except his arm, still held fast by one of his harness straps. On it was a tattoo, "Forget Me Not, Annie." The arm was buried in an unmarked grave at Drummond Hill cemetery. The rest of Stephens's body was never found.

Eight years passed before another daredevil challenged the falls. Having taken note of the damage suffered by barrel riders, this stuntman chose a unique vehicle for his trip.

Jean Lussier was a 35-year-old American of French-Canadian ancestry from Springfield, Massachusetts. He had worked as a salesman, a circus performer, and a racing car driver, and had become obsessed with a trip over Niagara after hearing about Charles Stephens's fatal journey.

After moving to Niagara Falls, New York, he began to plan his own plunge. Instead of a barrel, Lussier planned on using a huge rubber ball. He drew up the plans and approached two rubber companies in Akron, Ohio to build the giant sphere for him. Both turned him down, so he built it himself. About 2.5 metres in diameter, the ball was made of canvas stretched over a lightweight steel frame and filled with 32 rubber inner tubes. Inside the small opening was space for Lussier to sit while strapped into a

Red Hill Sr. (left) and Jean Lussier. The text on
Lussier's cap reads "Hero of Niagara."

harness. Lussier spent his entire life's savings —
$1500 — on the contraption, which was equipped
with 150 pounds of ballast and a system of valves to
allow fresh air to enter.

Although police had been alerted about Lussier's plans, he managed to evade detection on the afternoon of July 4, 1928. After being towed into the middle of the upper river, the ball was set free. On the way downstream the ballast tore loose. Two of the inner tubes burst with a loud bang, startling Lussier, but nothing could stop the momentum. Around 3 P.M., Jean Lussier's giant orange ball went over the falls. "I didn't even think. It all happened too fast," Lussier later told a reporter.

Red Hill Sr. rowed out to bring the ball to shore. It was a daunting task, as water leaked in through the ruptured side of the ball, and it bobbed awkwardly in the water. After some heavy going, Hill managed to tow it ashore. Then the thick rubber had to be cut apart in order to free Lussier. Looking dapper and only slightly bruised, Lussier emerged. His sister, who had travelled from Sherbrooke, Quebec to watch the stunt, greeted him with a hearty kiss on the cheek.

The stunt brought Lussier a bit of fame. He toured with the rubber ball, then later sold parts of the inner tubes to tourists for 50¢ apiece, and continued to sell pieces of inner tube long after the originals were gone. He settled permanently at Niagara Falls, New York, where he told the story of his adventure time and time again. He also started planning a second trip, this time over the perilous American Falls.

No daredevil had seriously considered tackling the American Falls, because of the huge quantity of rocks at the bottom of the drop. Jean Lussier felt it could be done, with the right equipment. He envisioned a three-layer ball, 3.5 metres in diameter, with the inner ball mounted on ball bearings, so it would stay upright all the time. He also planned for a 48-hour air supply and a radio communication system. But his dreams never materialized. He died in 1971.

The the next two men who attempted to ride over the falls — George Stathakis in 1930, and Red Hill Jr. in 1951 — met with disaster. However, the next man to challenge the falls tried an innovative approach.

Nathan Boya was exceptional in many ways. He was not interested in fame or fortune. Although he talked freely about his trip over the falls and his preparations for it, he kept the reasons a mystery and deliberately lied about his personal life.

A 30-year-old African-American man from the Bronx, Boya started thinking about a trip over Niagara Falls around 1951, while attending university in Switzerland. During the preparations for the stunt, he talked to Jean Lussier, asking the 1928 daredevil many questions about his own death-defying plunge.

With information garnered from Lussier and his

own research, Boya put together the *Plunge-o-Sphere*, a 1250-pound capsule made up of six layers of rubber and covered with steel. Table tennis balls and inflated cushions were inserted between the two sections to help keep it afloat, while 150 pounds of ballast went into a section below the cockpit.

Because Boya knew that air supply had been a problem for previous daredevils, he added six inflated inner tubes from truck tires to the inner chamber, intending to use the air in them in case of emergency. He also provided for several hours additional breathing time by purchasing a fireman's mask and canisters of air. In addition, he designed the opening of the sphere for quick access. He spent $5000, a small fortune, in his preparations, and at the last minute added one more expense. Boya hired a lawyer, who immediately asked if his client was planning to break the law. Still playing his cards close to his chest, Boya said he wouldn't be doing anything more serious than walking on the grass.

On July 15, 1961, he set off from a secret location on the American side. Few spectators were aware of Boya's plans, although he did enlist someone to tow him to the American side of the Niagara River.

The worst part of the journey was the ride through the rapids. Initially, Boya almost dozed off, possibly because of lack of air in the *Plunge-o-Sphere*. Then, as the water became more turbulent, he felt himself tossed about. At one point, when the capsule hit a rock, leaped a metre or so in the air then dropped back into the rapids, Boya thought he had gone over the falls. According to one report, he barely felt the 54-metre drop to the bottom of the falls at all. He still thought he was in the rapids, until he heard the motor of an approaching boat.

Moments later, his head popped out of the capsule. Boya waved to tourists on the *Maid of the Mist* and commented, "I made it all right, and I'm happy."

Almost immediately, he was arrested by a Niagara Parks Commission police officer. He was subsequently fined $113. Then he was taken to hospital, where doctors insisted he rest to forestall shock. Within an hour, he was talking to reporters.

The stories that emerged portrayed Boya as something of a mystery man. First of all, his name was not Nathan Boya but William Fitzgerald. Although he hinted that he was a salesman, and one reporter claimed he was a technical writer for IBM, it seemed he was a maintenance man for the company.

The reasons for his plunge were obscure. Jean Lussier, who had spoken to Fitzgerald on several occasions, spun a romantic tale about a love affair gone wrong. Fitzgerald had been jilted by his girlfriend, and the trip over the falls was a way of proving his love. That story was apparently fictitious, but Fitzgerald still wasn't revealing much to reporters. He refused to answer personal questions, telling reporters to talk to his attorney. He also turned down an offer to appear on the *Ed Sullivan Show*, the top television variety program of the time.

"I just made the trip for personal reasons," he declared. "I kept thinking about it, and finally decided to do it."

Historian Pierre Berton suggests Fitzgerald's motive was political. One reporter claimed his first words after emerging from the *Plunge-o-Sphere* were, "I have integrated the falls." The civil rights movement was gaining momentum in the American south, and Fitzgerald's alias resembled the name of the leader of Kenya's independence movement, Tom Mboya. If this was indeed the case, Fitzgerald did not speak at any length about it in the initial flurry of publicity.

William Fitzgerald continued his education, eventually earning a doctorate in behavioural sciences and sociology. In 1988 he announced he would take a second trip over the falls, but his wife apparently talked him out of it.

Chapter 6
Modern Daredevils

or a time it seemed Nathan Boya would be the last of the Niagara daredevils. No one made any serious attempt to go over the falls for 20 years, and after Jean Lussier's death in 1971, Boya, aka Fitzgerald, was the only man on earth who could speak about the experience first-hand. Then, in the 1980s, a former Czech soldier opened the floodgates. Between 1984 and 1995, nine different people challenged the falls. Amazingly, most lived to tell the tale.

Karel Soucek billed himself as the last of the Niagara daredevils. In July 1976, he tried to cross the whirlpool by riding a moped over the cables of the Spanish Aerocar. Six metres out, he hit a bolt and was knocked off his moped. Fortunately he was wearing a safety harness, which kept him from falling head-first into the whirlpool.

The following year, he tackled the whirlpool and rapids in a barrel. The trip, which took place on July 11, was made in a red, white, and blue barrel weighing 300 pounds. Inside, it was equipped with a bucket seat, a first aid kit, a crash helmet, and a case of beer.

The barrel went into the water just below Rainbow Bridge around 6 am. Everything went relatively well until it reached the whirlpool. There the barrel stuck for three hours. A rescue helicopter hovered over it, creating enough wind to blow it free. Once Soucek reached land, Niagara Parks Police arrested him.

On July 2, 1984, after eight years of dreaming and planning, Soucek was ready to ride over the falls. His barrel was a homemade contraption that cost $15,000. Just under 3 metres long and 1.5 metres around, it included a polyurethane cylinder encased in a riveted steel drum. Inside was a harness to hold Soucek in place and inner tubes to cushion him against the rough waters of the rapids. A Canadian flag was painted on the outside, along with Soucek's name. There were eye-holes for Soucek to see something of the outside world, as well as valves that could be opened to let air in.

Ambitious to make a name for himself as a professional stunt man, he had contacted the media. A crew of 15 was on hand to film the stunt.

To elude authorities, Soucek's team worked swiftly. Soucek was already in the barrel when they drove to the edge of the river a short distance above the falls and dropped the barrel into the water. By the time he went over the brink, the barrel was moving at an estimated speed of 120 kilometres per hour.

The barrel stuck at the foot of the falls. For 45 minutes, rescue teams tried but failed to reach it. They had no way of knowing whether Soucek had survived the fall. The two-way radio he carried had stopped working as the barrel began its descent.

After 45 minutes, the current shifted, and the barrel drifted free. Rescuers pulled it to shore. When Soucek emerged, his face was covered with blood. A flashlight had hit him in the forehead, causing a nasty gash. He had also chipped a tooth.

But he was ecstatic. "I knew my dream was coming true, finally. I was so happy."

He told reporters that the plunge over the falls "felt like a free fall out of a parachute before you

Karel Soucek in his bright red barrel at Niagara Falls

open your chute."

From Soucek's point of view, even the $500 fine he had to pay was worth it. "I just want to move into the big time now and do big stunts."

His wish came true, briefly. On January 19, 1985, he appeared before a crowd of 40,000 at the Houston Astrodome. Soucek had been paid $25,000 to recreate his trip over Niagara Falls, by dropping in a barrel from the roof of the Astrodome into a 3-metre tank of water.

This time something went terribly wrong. The barrel went into a spin as it was hoisted to the roof. Although the spinning stopped at the top, it started again as the barrel plummeted 55 metres towards the tank. Instead of hitting the water, it bounced off the side. Soucek was pulled from the wreckage with a fractured skull, massive chest injuries, and a crushed abdomen. He died a few hours later in a Houston hospital and was buried in Drummond Hill Cemetery, Niagara Falls.

In spite of Karel Soucek's tragic death, another ambitious would-be stuntman was inspired to tackle the falls the following year. Steve Trotter was 21, the youngest person to voluntarily challenge the might of Niagara. A part-time bartender who divided his time between Fort Lauderdale, Florida and Rhode Island, he had studied at a California stuntman school. There, he said, classmates had teased him, saying that no north-easterner could ever make it as a professional daredevil. Steve was determined to prove them wrong.

Up to that time, he had performed only one stunt in public — swinging from a rope at San Francisco's Golden Gate Bridge. For his Niagara challenge, he fused together two large plastic pickle barrels. The capsule measured 5 metres from one end to the other and about 2 metres around. Inside were two-way radios and two oxygen tanks. For extra protection, the outside of the barrel was covered with inner tubes and canvas.

By this time, Niagara Parks Police were going to great lengths to prevent stunts. As a result, daredevils and their friends had to work out how to elude authorities as well as plan the logistics of the stunt. In Trotter's case, everything went like clockwork. The 10-man support crew got the barrel into the water just above Terrapin Point. There was no interference from officials, as two of them tied themselves to lines and pushed Steve and his barrel into the middle of the river.

It was 8 A.M. on August 18, 1985. For the next several minutes, the crew kept in contact with Steve by radio. "I'm going for it!" he shouted as he approached the edge of the falls.

At 8:30, employees of the *Maid of the Mist* dragged the barrel ashore. Steve emerged, dressed only in print bathing trunks, white socks, and white running shoes.

"All right, we made it!" he crowed. His only injury was a scraped knee. Although charges were laid, Steve was unrepentant. "It was cool!" he told reporters. Later, while sipping champagne in his hotel room, he described the wild ride over the falls, "like the best roller-coaster ride you had when you were a 10 year old."

But others suggested that Steve's success was the result of sheer dumb luck. By coincidence, just five minutes before his barrel went over the falls, the Ontario Hydro control gates had been opened up to increase the flow of water in the river. The extra volume helped buoy up his barrel as he dropped to the river below.

Steve basked in the limelight that resulted from his stunt. As he told one reporter, he was more interested in getting recognition than in making money. He appeared on the Johnny Carson show and other popular television programs, and at one point bartended in Toronto as part of a publicity stunt. Then he faded into obscurity for 10 years, before returning to Niagara Falls determined to set a new record.

Meanwhile, other daredevils tried their luck. Since 1901, everyone who had gone over the falls had ridden in some variety of barrel or enclosed capsule. Jesse Sharp decided he would go down in history as the first man to paddle over the falls.

Sharp, a 28-year-old bachelor from Ocoee, Tennessee was an experienced whitewater kayaker. Supremely confident in his skills, he planned to ride the falls to the lower river, then paddle through the whirlpool and rapids down to Queenston. So sure was he of his ability to handle the raging water of Niagara that he made dinner reservations at a Queenston restaurant.

The kayak Jesse used measured almost 4 metres long and weighed 36 pounds. Like most modern stuntmen, he knew the value of publicity and had hired photographers and videographers. Jesse was planning a career as a professional stuntmen, and to make sure there was no mistake about who was in the kayak, he refused to wear a helmet so that his face could be clearly seen on tape.

At 1:50 on the afternoon of June 5, 1990, Jesse moved his red fibreglass kayak into the water about 900 metres above the falls. Stripped to the waist, he paddled smoothly towards the brink. Meanwhile, authorities had been alerted. In an attempt to run the

Jesse Sharp (highlighted by the circle) in his
kayak going over the falls

kayak aground, the flow of water at Ontario Hydro's
control dam was cut back to a trickle. But the action
came too late. There was still more than enough
water to keep the kayak afloat, right to the very edge
of the falls.

Below, spectators saw the red fibreglass kayak
emerge from the tumbling waters. Examined later, it

was found to have a small dent in one side. But Jesse Sharp had disappeared. No trace of his body was ever found.

Five years before Jesse Sharp's disastrous kayak ride, another daredevil challenged the falls. In 1985, David Munday became the second Canadian to go over Niagara Falls. Unlike Red Hill Jr., he was the first to survive the trip.

Munday was a 48-year-old mechanic who lived in Caistor Centre, a rural community east of the falls. His first attempt, on July 28 failed. A police officer spotted his silver and red barrel and alerted Ontario Hydro. The water in the river was lowered, dropping 1.5 metres within 3 minutes and trapping Munday in the river above the falls.

This failure on his first attempt only made Munday more determined. For a couple of weeks in September, he spent his time studying the movements of the police, learning when they took their coffee breaks, when they changed shifts, and when he could get his barrel into the river undetected. Knowing that they would be looking for him, he deliberately chose a cold, windy day — October 5.

At 8:15 A.M., Munday and his crew arrived at Table Rock. To avoid being recognized, he had travelled inside his double-walled steel barrel for the last

16 kilometres of the journey. Equipped with a two-way radio, a video camera to record the journey and breathing apparatus, the barrel had 25 centimetres of styrofoam between the two walls and weighed about 900 pounds. It was so bulky that the 12-man crew had trouble moving it from the truck into the water. When some tourists realized what was going on, they helped manoeuvre the bulky contraption.

From the time he went into the river until he reached the brink of the falls, Munday was in constant communication with his brother-in-law. When his brother-in-law told him, "Okay, you're going over. Good luck," Munday calmly replied "See you at the bottom." As he dropped over the falls, he counted slowly, trying to estimate the speed.

Knocked out momentarily when he hit the bottom, Munday quickly regained consciousness. "It was a rough ride. I'm just a little groggy," he reported over the radio. His neck and shoulders were bruised from his safety tank, and his left arm was swollen from crashing into an air tank. Otherwise, he was unharmed, although he spent 90 minutes at the foot of the falls before members of his support team rowed out, secured the barrel with a line and pulled Munday into the rescue boat. The barrel stayed behind.

Fined and placed on probation, Munday made it

clear he would try another stunt at Niagara, but waited until his probation period was up before making another attempt. This time, he decided to go through the Whirlpool Rapids. However, word got out, and on September 26, 1987, police spotted his barrel south of the Whirlpool Bridge. They confiscated it, putting a temporary stop to his plans.

Munday persisted, and on October 11, 1987 he floated through the Whirlpool Rapids in a steel barrel. Knowing the police would be watching, Munday's crew worked quickly to unload the barrel from a truck, close the hatch, and toss it into the river. Inside, the equipment was minimal — a black hockey helmet, a couple of pillows, and a two-way radio. There was no extra air supply, and Munday later estimated he had perhaps 15 minutes of air.

Fortunately everything went according to plan, although the ride was so rough that Munday was almost sick to his stomach. A member of his crew got a rope around the barrel, pulled it to shore, and the hatch was opened.

"As soon as I caught my breath, I just ran," Munday later told a reporter. "I didn't want to get caught." Although he eluded police, he turned himself in later that night.

On November 12th, 1987, Munday was fined

$500 at Niagara Falls Ontario Provincial Court and given 2 years' probation. But nothing could cure Dave Munday of his obsession with the falls. He was offended by comments that the barrel he had used in his first ride over the precipice had been so high-tech that the trip posed no risk at all. So, on July 5, 1990, he made a second attempt in his "no frills barrel," a 394-pound container. This time, it jammed on the brink of the falls. Because Munday had not packed any extra air, he was in danger of suffocating. To allow him to breathe, the water in the upper river was lowered while rescuers from the Niagara Parks Police struggled for two and a half hours to pull the barrel to shore with a sturdy cable. Munday was charged with stunting without permission, and fined $4000 plus $375 expenses, less than half the maximum. And again he was placed on probation.

Munday bided his time, all the while planning his next trip over the falls. The day came on September 27, 1993. This time, his vehicle of choice was a red-and-white steel barrel made from an old diving bell and decorated with maple leaves. Just over a metre in diameter, it was lined with 5 centimetres of padding. Notably absent were air tanks and radio, as well as any space to move around.

The small barrel went into the water a short

distance above the falls, where it moved rapidly to the edge. The plunge took about 5 seconds. Three-quarters of an hour later, Dave Munday emerged from the barrel. He had just made the record books, becoming the first person to go over the falls twice and survive. Another record-breaking stunt was performed by two Canadians, 42-year-old Peter DiBernardi of Niagara Falls, a former racing car driver, and 24-year-old Jeffrey Petkovic, a student at the University of Ottawa. In 1989 they made history as the first pair to ride the falls.

DiBernardi was the mastermind behind this stunt. A reformed abuser of prescription drugs, he wanted to send a message to young people that going over Niagara Falls in a barrel was safer than getting hooked on drugs. Initially, another man had agreed to go over the falls with him, but he backed out a few weeks earlier.

By this time, DiBernardi already had invested in a $1500 steel-plated barrel. Measuring 3.5 metres long and 1.5 metres around, the barrel had a keel to help with steering. It was also big enough for the two men to lie inside head to head. In addition to an air supply and a two-way radio, the barrel was equipped with two Plexiglass windows, so the passengers could watch the water as they tumbled over the falls. The outside of the barrel was painted bright yellow, and emblazoned with the slogan, "Don't Put Yourself on the Edge — Drugs Kill."

The barrel went into the water just 60 metres from the edge of the falls and was quickly recovered at the base of the falls and pulled to the *Maid of the Mist* dock. Petkovic, who had been drinking, emerged wearing a necktie, cowboy boots, and nothing else. The pair was later fined for performing a stunt without permission and for trespassing.

The following year, DiBernardi planned a second stunt, this time a trip over the rocky American Falls in a yellow styrofoam ball. The plans fell apart when New York State Parks Police stopped the truck carrying the contraption.

In the late spring of 1995, after a 10 year absence, Steve Trotter returned to Niagara Falls. This time his girlfriend, 29-year-old Lori Martin of Atlanta, Georgia accompanied him. Their plan was to become the first man-and-woman team to conquer the falls.

For his 1995 stunt, Steve Trotter's preparations were somewhat more elaborate than they had been 10 years earlier. His barrel was made from two water heater tanks welded together and coated with Kevlar. Inside the 3.5-metre structure were four oxygen tanks. The whole thing weighed about 900 pounds and cost approximately $19,000 U.S. to build — money provided by a Florida investment banker.

It was Father's Day, June 18, 1995. At approximately 9:30 A.M., the barrel was put into the water about 90 metres above the Horseshoe Falls. Moments later, it was caught in the huge pile of rocks at the base of the falls.

While Steve's 74-year-old father watched, emergency rescue workers from the Niagara Falls Fire Department, Niagara Parks Police, and Niagara Falls Ambulance Service rushed to the scene. Some of them climbed over the guard rail outside one of the observation tunnels under Table Rock pavilion, tied the barrel to keep it from dropping any farther, and pulled Trotter and Martin to safety. The pair were taken to hospital suffering from minor bruises, and were then arrested for the stunt. Released on bail, Lori pleaded guilty and was fined $2000. Steve, who spent two weeks in jail, was fined $5000 and was also required to pay $515 for his hospital treatment. In addition, he paid the costs of removing the barrel, which stayed where it had landed for nine days until it was lifted away by a crane.

Although there was considerable media interest in Steve and Lori's stunt, there was also criticism. The harshest words came from Niagara Falls authorities, who pointed out that at least 20 members of emergency rescue teams had risked their lives to save two individuals whose only interest was a moment of glory.

Yet neither criticism nor logic seemed capable of stopping determined daredevils. A little more than three months after Steve Trotter and Lori Martin made their semi-successful plunge, Robert Overacker bet his life against the power of the falls and lost.

A 39-year-old married man, Overacker hailed from Camarillo, Texas. Like Steven Trotter, he had also attended a California stunt school. Although he said he wanted to call attention to the plight of the homeless, he had been preparing his stunt for seven years.

Overacker planned to ride a jet ski to the brink of the falls, launch a rocket-propelled parachute, and then glide to the river below.

He had actually planned the stunt once before, but friends had sabotaged his equipment. This time, while his brother and a friend watched, he made a successful start just after 12:35 P.M. on October 1, 1995. But the rocket failed. The parachute did not open and Overacker dropped to his death at the foot of Niagara Falls.

Epilogue

Ultimately, daredevils are a tiny minority of visitors to the falls. Since 1829, when Sam Patch began his famous dives, fewer than 100 individuals have publicly challenged the might of Niagara. Of these, the people who chose to ride over the falls may be considered the elite. Their names — Annie Taylor, Bobby Leach, Charles Stephens, Jean Lussier, George Stathakis, Red Hill Jr., Nathan Boya, Karel Soucek, David Munday, Jeffrey Petkovic, Peter Dibernardi, Jessie Sharp, Lori Martin, Robert Overacker and Kirk Jones — will forever be associated with one of the most stupendous natural wonders of the world.

When this book was written in May 2003, Steve Trotter and Lori Martin were unofficially the last of the Niagara daredevils. As predicted, they have not kept that title. On Monday, October 20, 2003, Kirk Jones, a 40-year-old from Michigan, became the 13th man and 15th individual to deliberately go over the falls. Unlike his predecessors, he had no equipment — no barrel, no life jacket, no kayak. He simply climbed over a wrought-iron barricade and down an embankment, stepped into the water and let the power of the Niagara sweep him along. He survived the plunge with only minor bruises.

Jones's survival was nothing short of miraculous. Of the 13 men and two women who rode the falls, five died outright. A sixth, Karel Soucek, was killed trying to re-create his stunt. The odds, while slightly in favour of the daredevils, are not good. And yet both David Munday and Steve Trotter returned to defy Niagara a second time, and both survived.

Although hefty fines and strict surveillance have drastically cut down stunting at Niagara, the falls still exert a pull on thrill seekers.

No one is quite certain why Niagara has such a tremendous attraction for visitors and risk takers. What is known is that the attraction is often fatal. Since tourists first began flocking to the falls in the early 1800s, more than 5000 people have chosen to commit suicide there.

Self-destruction may not have been foremost in the minds of Niagara daredevils, but there is no doubt they were acutely aware of the falls' attraction. Whether they were seeking money, fame, or personal fulfilment, they all believed Niagara held the answers. For them, the falls were a magnificent obsession that could not be ignored.

Select Bibliography

Berton, Pierre. *Niagara: A History of the Falls.* Toronto: McClelland & Stewart Inc., 1994.

Peacock, Shane. *The Great Farini: The High-Wire Life of William Hunt.* Toronto: Penguin Books Canada Ltd, 1995

Stephenson, William. *Dawn of the Nation 1860-1870.* Toronto: N.S.L. Natural Science of Canada Limited, 1977.

Acknowledgments

The author acknowledges two excellent sources on the history of Niagara Falls which proved invaluable for many of the quotes contained in this book: the entertaining *Niagara: A History of the Falls* by Pierre Burton, and the fascinating article "Sam Patch—A Tremendous Jump" which appeared in *Sketches of Canada and the United States* (London, 1833). The author would also like to acknowledge the excellent resource provided by past editions of such regional and national newspapers as *The Globe and Mail,* the *Colonial Advocate,* and *The Toronto Star.* The reports from these papers provide a blow-by-blow account of many of the events described in this book.

Photograph Credits

Cover: Anna Edson Taylor (Niagara Falls (Ontario) Public Library); **Niagara Falls (Ontario) Public Library:** pages 19, 30, 35, 52, 80, 85, 91, 100, 105.

About the Author

Cheryl MacDonald has been writing on historical topics for nearly 30 years. Her work has appeared in numerous magazines, including *The Beaver* and *Maclean's*, and she has written a number of books, mostly relating various aspects of southern Ontario history.

Cheryl holds history degrees from the University of Waterloo and McMaster University and is currently pursuing graduate studies. A grandmother of two, she lives on a large rural property close to Lake Erie and about 90 minutes west of Niagara Falls.

OTHER AMAZING STORIES

These titles are available wherever you buy books. If you have trouble finding the book you want, call the Altitude order desk at 1-800-957-6888, e-mail your request to: orderdesk@altitudepublishing.com or visit our Web site at www.amazingstories.ca

New AMAZING STORIES titles are published every month. If you would like more information, e-mail your name and mailing address to: amazingstories@altitudepublishing.com.